The red doll
and other stories

The red doll page 2

The secret of the castle
page 10

The circus boy page 19

Nelson

The red doll

Maria was sad. It was wet and she had to play inside.
"What can I do?" she said.
"Here is a box of old toys," said Mum.

Maria looked in the box.
She saw an old paint box
but no paint brush.
She saw a book with
lots of pages missing.
At the bottom of the box
she found a red doll made of wood.

Maria looked at the doll.
She shook it.
"Can you keep a secret?"
said the doll.
"Turn my middle and you will see
another doll just like me."

Maria turned the doll's middle and out fell another doll.
"Why do you smile?" said Maria.
"Can you keep a secret?"
said the doll.
"Turn my middle and you will see another doll just like me."

Maria turned the doll's middle and out fell another doll.
"Why do you sing?" said Maria.
"Can you keep a secret?"
said the doll.
"Turn my middle and you will see another doll just like me."

Maria turned the doll's middle and another doll fell out.
"Why are you sad?" said Maria.
"My baby is lost," said the doll.

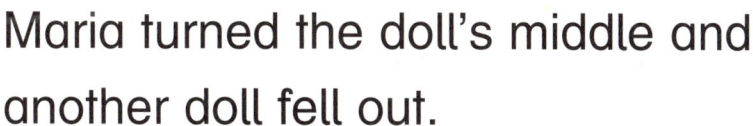

Maria turned the doll's middle but there was no baby doll inside.
"Don't be sad," she said.
"Your baby can't be far away."

Maria looked in the box.
In the corner she found
the baby doll asleep in
a little bed.
"I put her there when I was
a little girl," said Mum.
"It was wet and I had to play inside."

The secret of the castle

"Let's have a picnic," said Mum.
"Where shall we go?"
"Let's go to the castle," said Dad.
"It's the last time we can go there.
They are going to shut it up."

Tara and Ramu helped pack the
picnic and they all set off
in the car.
At the gate of the castle
Dad got four tickets.
"The castle will soon be shut,"
said the gate man.
"There is no money to
mend the castle."

Tara and Ramu ran inside.

"Let's hide," said Tara.

"In here," said Ramu.

"Dad won't look in here."

Tara pulled the door shut.
"Look out," said Ramu.
"That door is very old.
Can you open it?"
"No, I can't," said Tara.
"What shall we do?"

"Let's bang on the door.
Dad will hear us," said Ramu.
They banged and banged but
no one came.
Ramu sat down on a stone.

The stone moved.
"Come and help push, Tara," said Ramu.
"Look what I can see."
They saw a small hole under the stone.
"What's that in the hole?" said Tara.

Ramu put his hand in the hole.
He took out an old book.
"All the letters are painted in gold,"
said Tara.
Just then Dad opened the door.

"Look at this book.
It was in this hole," said Ramu.
"We must take it to the gate man,"
said Dad.
The man at the gate looked
at the book.

"How did you find it?" he said.
"This book will save the castle.
We will sell it and then
we won't have to shut the castle."
"Then we can have a picnic here
again," said Mum.
"What will you two find next time?"

The circus boy

Jim had a cold.
"You must stay in bed," said Mum.
"Look at this book about a circus."
Jim looked at the pictures of
the circus and the ring master.
His eyes closed and he fell asleep.

"Welcome to the circus,"
said the ring master.
The music played and
the elephants came into the ring.
Jim was riding on the first elephant.
The elephants went round the ring.

Then the horses came into the ring.
Jim was riding on a big black horse.
The horses went round and
round the ring.
The crowd clapped and clapped.

Now Jim was a juggler.
He had ten balls in the air.
He walked across a rope and jumped through a hoop.
He did not drop the balls.

Then the clowns came into the ring.
Now Jim was a clown.
He had a blue and white coat and
a red nose.
He ran round and round the ring with
the other clowns.
The crowd clapped and clapped.

One clown got hold of
Jim's arm and shook him hard.
"Wake up, Jim," said Mum.
"You look just like a clown with
your red nose," she said.
And so he did.